EASTERN STEAM DAYS REMEMBERED

There is just over a year of service life remaining for 60032 *Gannet*, seen here climbing through Holloway with a northbound passenger working on 18 August 1962. (Gerald T. Robinson)

EASTERN STEAM DAYS REMEMBERED

Kevin Derrick

AMBERLEY

This edition first published 2017

Amberley Publishing
The Hill, Stroud
Gloucestershire, GL5 4EP

www.amberley-books.com

ISBN 978 1 4456 6989 2 (print)
ISBN 978 1 4456 6990 8 (ebook)

British Library Cataloguing in Publication Data.
A catalogue record for this book is available from the British Library.

Origination by Amberley Publishing.
Printed in the UK.

Contents

Preface

We continue with the Steam Days Remembered series to enjoy a leisurely ramble back around both the Eastern and North Eastern regions during the 1950s and 1960s in this volume. To conclude the trilogy of reminiscences begun by Roger Stanton in the first two volumes of *London Steam Days Remembered*, we journey towards the eastern counties of the Midlands and far beyond. Perhaps you too will pick up a few similarities, maybe, to your own memories of those now distant and far off times as we venture through this collection together, journeying back into that bygone steam-laden era.

If we visited many of the locations featured here today we would be hard pushed to recognise exactly where each cameraman was standing as they fired the shutter, such have been the degree of changes which have ravaged both the railways and our countryside in the passing fifty or so years. Today, while we may be whisked quietly along the East Coast Main Line underneath overhead wires by electric traction in some comfort, many of us would still wish to journey back in time, to enjoy life as it was once again in the days of everyday steam once more.

So we should give thanks to all those who took such shots and have been kind enough to allow us to see their work published today, to share our yearnings for the past.

Kevin Derrick
Inverness, 2014

Introduction – Steam, Fishing, Holidays and Work Tales

Welcome to part three of my trilogy. Spotting wasn't just a matter of standing on a platform end or a bridge, as it was possible to travel on shed bashes and weave other activities into spotting as well, including other hobbies, holidays and even work!

Shed Bashes

Several of my local sheds had been visited, including Rugby and Leicester, but in about 1960 a bloke called Brian (W. B.) Alexander who lived locally promoted a spotting club and the first trip proposed was to Manchester. Surprisingly this provoked a somewhat muted response but on reflection I now realise that Manchester wasn't considered a major 'go to' for spotting. However, eventually, Brian coerced enough people to commit to going, so he duly booked a coach from the local Midland Red garage. From memory this was a C1, KHA 303. No M1 motorway in those days so off we went via Derby and the A6. First shed visited was 9B Stockport at about 7.30 in the morning! I was always convinced that we had called in at 17C Rowsley on our way through the Peak District but I have made contact recently with an old spotting mate and, through one of his friends, we now have notes of the sheds visited and locos seen on that trip, and there is no mention of Rowsley. We'd already been round Rugby that morning at about 4.00 a.m., as it was rumoured a Canklow 8F was in town. It's a fair bet that most of us would have copped 90 per cent plus of what we saw that day. I'd estimate we saw over 700 locos in that trip and it set the agenda for many more trips. Highlights of that trip are too many to really do justice to. Most of the passenger locos we would have already seen through Rugby but almost all the freight engines were cops. Bolton shed offered the only Fowler 7Fs I ever saw; No. 49668 was one of them but the other number is long forgotten. At Bury, Brian photographed six or seven of us standing by the buffer-beam of No. 42700, which is now part of the National Collection. This photograph turned up in *Steam World* several years ago as part of the 'Where are they now?' feature. We also noted some of the last L&Y 0-6-0 tender locos at Oldham Lees depot and at Longsight, for those interested in such things, we also noted one of the first AC electrics, E3303. Oddly enough our Midland Red coach also carried the same number. We had shed passes for every shed in the district except Gorton, but Brian talked his way in there as well and we also did the works. This raised the ethics of whether it is fair to allow a cop when you have only seen a cab panel carrying a number as we saw several such. I remember the weather to have been appalling but with a few cases of beer on the back seat a good day was had by all.

This led to more trips being arranged as soon as possible and eventually each trip became a sell-out very quickly. The one I was really keen on was to the Leeds area and I remember I nearly stuffed it up by missing the bus (someone nearly always did). First call was at 55D Royston to bag their rare 8Fs and then on to Normanton before hitting Leeds and their big sheds Holbeck, Farnley (for some rare Jubes) and Copley Hill. Again, as at Gorton, we didn't have a permit but access was easily obtained and almost the first loco seen standing in the shed yard was No. 60038 *Firdaussi*, a rare A3. Many of the Holbeck Jubilees were copped but most of the Royal Scots were missing. Initially this was a big disappointment but we were told that since dieselisation they had all been sent to 56D Mirfield and we would almost certainly see them later in the day, which we did. Neville Hill and Stourton were also visited. The reserved for preservation Class N7 No. 69621 was in Neville Hill and we caught up with several more A3 cops at Ardsley shed. A visit was also made to Wakefield and we then went over to Bradford and visited the old GN shed of Hammerton Street, which had been converted into a diesel multiple unit shed. The main steam sheds were Low Moor and Manningham, which were still very busy. To round off the day we went to Huddersfield, Sowerby Bridge and Mirfield. Another brilliant day with probably 600 or 700 cops. Little did I know that in 1977 I'd be living in Wakefield and catch up on a lot of these places during my normal business day as a lot of railway land was converted to trading and industrial estates. It was very hard to see where the railway activity had been at places like Low Moor but large parts of Holbeck remained largely unchanged.

Other trips included the Nottingham/Sheffield and Doncaster areas but strangely London remained off the agenda for a long time. I can now reason that Brian was running the club to suit his own ends and as he'd done London a few times he wasn't about to do it again just for us, but eventually it came around. As usual we did it the roundabout way. First shed was 14E Bedford (some of the last working examples of Midland 3Fs), then on to Hitchen, now devoid of steam but home to some diesels; Hatfield was similar and then we hit London and its big sheds. Devons Road was visited amongst the minnows, with again no steam but lots of D8xxx. By the time we'd been round Camden, the Cross, Willesden, etc. and time was running out, as was daylight! We'd been to Neasden just to see and photograph an empty shed but did the now closed Kentish Town and found it still full of steam, ironically. Cricklewood had a York V2 on shed as it was now servicing locos off the GC. Old Oak Common, sadly, was still full of withdrawn Kings and Castles with no plates or names and I have to admit I thought the end to spotting was not far away. It was dark by the time we got to Nine Elms and we were refused entry so home we went. One last stop was made for sausage, egg and chips at a café called the Busy Bee on the Edgware Road, I believe, where we saw hundreds of bikies. Wall-to-wall Bonnevilles with not a Japanese job in sight! The only major shed not on the agenda was 30A Stratford. Again, no permit was available and it remained the only London shed I never visited but as steam was almost gone from the Great Eastern section I wasn't much bothered.

Some independent trips were made both by train and by car if you could find anyone who owned one! One of my mates, Bob Rainbow, had an uncle who was an assistant station master at Crewe so the correct arrangements were made to visit. We started by catching a local to Birmingham which went via the now closed Leamington line and the Kenilworth Junction–Berkswell Loop. Saltley shed was visited before heading off to New Street and a Crewe train. We did the lot at Crewe, including the works and Gresty Lane, and were heading home via the direct Trent Valley service when we discovered No. 45581 *Bihar and Orissa* was on a running-in turn back to New Street. This was too good to miss so back to Birmingham we went, and as an encore we decided we may as well bag Tyseley and Aston sheds to close a good day.

Shortly after I managed to bag the last seat in Brian's car for a Sunday trip to Market Harborough, March, New England, Wellingborough, Kettering and finally Northampton. It was an incident-filled day as we were chased by the police at March and nearly got ourselves run over at Northampton.

The Liverpool area was visited by train one Easter Sunday. The shed-master tried to arrest all eight of us at Bank Hall but four of us ran away and jumped on a bus to escape. Walton on the Hill had twenty odd locos on but was locked up and the only way in was over a fence with barbed wire, but in we went and then on to a place called Speke which made the outer Moscow suburbs look good! Edge Hill was brilliant and then over to Birkenhead where No. 92231 with a 71A shed plate was noted. Leaving the shed, the locals decided we needed pelting with rocks. And so back to Lime Street to catch up with the others who got caught and fined for the Bank Hall incident.

The local spotting club sort of staggered on, with the end coming when we couldn't get enough to go on a weekend visit covering Gloucester, Bristol and all of South Wales. With the rapid withdrawal of the passenger classes it was not possible to get enough people to make it pay.

Other Hobbies

I've already mentioned a few occasions where I was able to combine my fishing with some spotting, with some interesting results. There were many fishing locations around Rugby as we had the River Avon, the Oxford Canal and many lakes and ponds. One of my favourite places was the reach above Rugby up to Newton. For a small river it offered excellent sport and the Great Central could be seen from much of it. The GC ran on a high embankment before crossing the Oxford Canal on the large viaduct previously mentioned. The railway crossed the river on a large blue brick structure that still exists but everything else is largely gone as the fields are now built on. Further north we used the GC as access to the gravel pits at Shawell as the owners wouldn't allow fishing, but we would dump our bikes in the bushes where the GC crossed Watling Street (A5) and walk up the track. The pits were full of crucian carp, rudd and roach. Many stretches of the Oxford Canal offered views of the GC and in the Barby Lane area one could watch these workings at speed as they worked up into the Northampton uplands heading south.

One of my school pals, Trevor Roach, invited me one day over to his house at Willoughby to fish the infant River Leam. Again, this small, almost unfished stream held a good head of roach, chub, dace, perch and even the odd trout. Access was down his back garden, over the fence and down the track towards Woodford. On this first trip we hadn't gone far when we saw a Woodford WD on a P-way train. No one seemed too excited to see three kids walking down the four foot and greetings were exchanged, the driver telling us we were wasting our time in such a little brook. I fished this area many times up to the end of steam and watched the Yorks and the many 'runners' belting south. Some time ago I wrote to Colin Walker, who must be the photographic expert on the GC, to see if he had an appropriate photograph of Willoughby viaduct but on reply he said it was the only structure he never shot as access was so hard. Right at the end of the GC I also remember fishing a club match on the Oxford at the old Navigation Inn and successive north-bound services were hauled by No. 45565 *Victoria* and No. 62049, a Class K1 from York. Anything could turn up at the end of steam!

The railway was also used to quite extensively to go fishing. From 1959 onwards we used the GC to go to Leicester to fish the famous 'Straight', which was a canalised section of the River Soar and the Grand Union Canal. It was a warm water stretch as the cooling towers from Leicester power station emptied into it under Walnut Street bridge. It was excellent fishing at all times of the year for carp, tench and roach.

Leicester Central shed backed on to the canal up by Kings Common lock so I usually had a look in to see what was 'on'. We would catch the 06.05 from Rugby Central, which was a workman's train from Woodford to Leicester, usually headed by one of Woodford's decrepit B1s; No. 61206 was a regular for quite a while. Usually it would still be dark on arrival and if there was no evidence of hot water from the power station, breakfast would be taken in the café round at St Margarets bus station. Once we started fishing there would be regular noises in the background as a 9F was opened up after passing Leicester South Goods. The site of Leicester South became Berry's scrap yard, famous for the scrapping of many diesels and the heap of Class 25s that became quite a local landmark.

Northampton was also regularly visited to fish the River Nene, again down by the local power station. In the winter of 1962/63 these were virtually the only places left un-frozen to fish for miles. The LNW line to Peterborough was visible for miles as it followed the Nene Valley and we were able to note many workings, both freight and passenger. Just outside Northampton the branch to Bedford turned east and we used the trains to fish at Olney on the River Ouse. Although I saw Ivatts in use on the local train service, I never travelled behind one, but the freight service used the Bedford 3Fs and once Black Five No. 45238 was seen. We always got a DMU on the morning train. All these areas have changed dramatically. The station at Olney has disappeared to be replaced by an estate of executive-style dwellings. The bridge over the river carrying the trackbed was removed 'as dangerous', which is news to me as I've driven my company car over it!

A trip was made to Kelso in 1962 for a holiday, fishing on the famous River Tweed. As well as being one of the most famous salmon rivers in the world, the river also held a huge head of big roach plus dace, trout and grayling. John Snelson and I went up in his Reliant Robin and some railway activity was noted in the Newcastle area on the way through, but by Tuesday it was obvious that the fishing was 'not good' so I decided to catch the morning bus to Berwick-upon-Tweed having missed the morning train. The day was spent on Berwick station noting lots of steam, including No. 60023 *Sea Eagle* on a car carrier working. I also met a lad from Doncaster who was staying with his aunt on holiday, and we decided to meet again on Thursday and take an excursion to Edinburgh, more of which anon. We tried to bunk Tweedmouth but to no avail, although we did note No. 60129 *Guy Mannering* in the yard. On the Thursday I caught the morning train from St Boswells, which was hauled by No. 78049. I was the only passenger in the single coach both ways and still kick myself I didn't go for the cab-ride. The Tweed Valley line was a beautiful trip following the river for much of the way. Arrival at Berwick was shortly to be followed by No. 60036 *Colombo* pulling in with the excursion and off we went. Arrival at Haymarket was brilliant. J38s and other types never previously seen abounded and after some time on Waverley we took off to Princes Street and Dalry Road shed. Getting blasé by now, we headed off to Haymarket and apart from the spotting couldn't get over how friendly everyone was. Not at all like English shed foremen. Haymarket completed we headed for the last Edinburgh shed at St Margarets, where once again the welcome was friendly. Then it was back to Waverley for a mid-afternoon semi-fast to Berwick as I had to catch the afternoon working to Kelso; No. 78047 took me back and I often wondered where No. 78049 went to as there was no traffic over the Tweed Valley between the two passenger workings. My mate John didn't share my enthusiasm for trains and tried to claim a big catch of roach that day but I never believed him!

The other area visited extensively was the Cherwell Valley between Banbury and Oxford, with Aynho and Upper Heyford being favourites. Again the Oxford Canal, River Cherwell and the GWR line closely followed each other down the valley. The last steam workings I saw in the area were in late 1965 while fishing behind Heyford church. Battered Halls and 9Fs with numbers roughly painted on their cab-sides were the order of the day. Oddly enough, my final trip down the Cherwell, before moving to live in Yorkshire, was in March 1977 and I witnessed the final workings of the Class 52 Westerns on the Paddington–Birmingham service, but to New Street and not Snow Hill by now. I also caught a lot less this time!

My final fishing memory for you is fishing the Hampshire Avon at Christchurch in the early 1960s, with Bulleids and Standards being the main locos seen, but the York–Bournemouth still brought a Banbury Hall south on a daily working. I also lost a huge barbell on this trip so this is the story of the one that got away!

Holidays

All holidays pre-1964 had to have some railway content or they were not a lot of good! Following some kind of date order, I suppose the first one I really remember was to East Anglia in dad's old Morris Commercial van. We camped near Felixstowe and I copped half a dozen L1s on Ipswich–Felixstowe locals on the first afternoon. I remember copping No. 65460 near Saxmundham but most of the rest is lost, except seeing some of the final workings of Holden's F5 and F6 classes near Cromer.

The following year Devon and Cornwall were visited, to stay with dad's brother and his family in Plympton. It didn't take long to find the GWR main line and Laira shed but access to the latter was impossible although much could still be seen from the road. Plymouth Friary remained a mystery as I couldn't persuade my parents to take me to the shed and station but I did see several ex-SR locos at Plymouth North Road, including No. 34037 *Clovelly*. GWR traffic was all steam still and Kings and Castles remained on front-line duties. For some reason dad went home early and we returned home by train and were King-hauled as far as Westbury. North Road memories that morning included No. 73025, from Swindon. From Westbury we eventually turned up in Banbury to catch a connection to Rugby via the GC hauled by a K3.

We often went back to Spalding and Holbeach where I was born and I remember one day spending quite a bit of time on Spalding station while my parents went to see someone. There was still plenty of steam about and the day's highlight was No. 61657 *Doncaster Rovers* on a GN and GE joint service. I also remember lots of Ivatts as Boston shed now had some to replace their ex-GN K2s. Also had a strange incident one day while returning from a fishing competition on the Welland. The road from Spalding to Deeping crosses the GN Peterborough line and in the distance I could see a B1 light engine heading south away from us. Steam had long since finished in this part of the world and I can only think it was one of the last B1s, kept for steam heating and Departmental use, being moved to New England.

The final steam holiday story concerns my first trip to Ireland for a two-week fishing holiday. We left Rugby late Friday afternoon on a relief to the Irish Mail behind No. 45646 *Napier* which wandered all around the Black Country before re-joining civilisation at Stafford where it finally expired, to be replaced by 90348, a wandering WD from 56A Wakefield. This 'race-horse' pulled us over to Crewe, where we were all told to decant from that train and get on to an eight-car DMU for the onward trip to Holyhead. What a drama. However the best bit of the trip was to cop several Jinties, still pottering about at Holyhead harbour. In those days Dun Laoghaire harbour was still connected by rail to Dublin Westland Row so the train was again used. We stayed at Belturbet in County Cavan and this little town was served by CIE and the now closed Cavan & Leitrim narrow gauge line and between knocking out 5lb bream and drinking Smithwick's finest I explored what remained of the Cavan & Leitrim.

Work

I suppose it's fitting to close this epistle with a memory of the end of steam in Britain. I was working for the chief estimator of a civil engineering company and one day we rather cut it fine for delivery of a tender to Ove Arup, Consulting Engineers in Manchester. So I was driven down to Coventry station and told, 'This has to be there before 12 noon.' BR did it's best to make sure it didn't happen but after a quick trip down Deansgate, where I was able to say to the taxi driver those immortal words, we got there with ten minutes to spare. Back on Piccadilly station I spent the rest of the day watching the last working steam I ever saw, mainly a collection of Black Fives and occasional 8Fs.

I did use the railway extensively at this time for site visits to Bristol and South Wales but that's another story as steam was just history in those areas by this time and all those trips were diesel-hauled and the general railway scene was contracting and was one of sadness at the passing of an era.

Roger Stanton
West Australia 2014

Digging in hard for the climb through South Pelaw in the mid-1960s was No. 92063, with another of the Tyne Dock allocated Class 9Fs banking hard behind with another of the Consett iron ore workings. (Noel Marrison)

Fitted with a self-weighing tender, a recently ex-works Class B1 No. 61258 ambles along between the various loops along the ECML near Retford around 1961. Steam's reign was starting to give way to the new diesel deliveries each and every month for the next few years. (Strathwood Library Collection)

One of the Cravens-built DMUs rattles away alongside another recently ex-works Class B1, No. 61348, at Spalding Town in former Great Northern Railway territory in October 1961. (Colour Rail)

The fireman must be busy with his firebox as Class 9F No. 92143 hurries a fish train along the East Coast Main Line near Retford in 1962. (Strathwood Library Collection)

It's a cold and frosty start to 1967 at Wakefield Kirkgate as Ivatt Class 4MT No. 43070 shunts parcels traffic as one of the then regular 'Dub Dee' 2-8-0s, No. 90620, approaches around the curves with a coal train on 2 January. (Bill Wright)

The Butlins headboard affixed to Class B1 No. 61302, standing at Boston at the start of the 1960s, meant it would be one of a number of trains that Saturday transferring holiday makers to and from Billy Butlin's camp at Skegness. What a delightful collection of ironwork to be enjoyed in this view around this spacious station. (Colour Rail)

Through Eastern Links

No. 60017 *Silver Fox* would most likely be a favourite Class A4 for many, because of the splendid fox motif affixed to its flanks in the same style as those fitted to the nameplates of the Class D49/2 Hunts. Today it is seen superbly turned out in the morning sunshine at Top Shed for today's 10.00 departure from Kings Cross bound for Edinburgh. (Strathwood Library Collection)

Fellow enthusiasts lend a helping hand to turn Class B1 No. 61173 on Nottingham Victoria's turntable on the last day of steam running to Marylebone on 3 September 1966. From tomorrow it will be DMUs for the 126-mile route that neither the Eastern Region nor the London Midland Region wanted to keep open. (Strathwood Library Collection)

Entering service in May 1948 from Darlington Works to a design by Edward Thompson, Class L1 No. 67715 would enjoy an amazingly short service life of just under fourteen years. No wonder it seems as though we see the signs for the future at Stratford alongside the mainline station on 7 June 1959. (Late Norman Browne/ Strathwood Library Collection)

The rich blue-lined blue livery adorning one of Liverpool Street's regular pilots, Class J69/1 No. 68619, in this view from 1960 harks back to this busy terminus in Great Eastern Railway days. The fact that a new Brush Type 2 stands alongside brings us also to the last year of the 0-6-0T's fifty-seven-year service life. (Strathwood Library Collection)

The same plucky little Class J69/1 is on duty again at Liverpool Street a few months beforehand on 26 October 1959, as Britannia No. 70039 *Sir Christopher Wren* alongside dwarfs it with the waiting 09.30 departure for Ipswich and Norwich named service, which would be extended to Cromer in the summer timetables. (Douglas Twibble)

One of the longest lived of the 127 Class J15s that came into British Railways' service would be No. 65445, which was built at Stratford Works by the Great Eastern Railway in 1899. It was withdrawn ten months after this view was taken in the large marshalling yard at Temple Mills on 7 October 1961. (Late Vincent Heckford/ Strathwood Library Collection)

Keeping a keen lookout while running fast through the freezing fog in the winter of 1962/3 would be hard on the crew of Class V2 No. 60894 as they race through St Neots with an up fish train for London. (Late Vincent Heckford/Strathwood Library Collection)

Most likely taken that same morning, on 29 December 1962, was this shot of Class L1 No. 67800 getting away from Bingham on what could well have been the Thompson locomotive's last working as it was withdrawn at the year's end. (Colour Rail)

Sheffield was an important source of traffic to both the Eastern Region and the London Midland Region, as here at Sheffield Midland in 1964 as the hiss of leaking steam from the Peak's train heating and the Ivatt Class 2MT, No. 46465, help to drown out the sound of the Sulzer diesel. (Strathwood Library Collection)

Running slowly through the platform roads at Peterborough in 1960, in what was a great bottleneck for the ECML, was Class 9F No. 92140. (Strathwood Library collection)

Most of the ninety-strong Holden-designed Class J17s had been withdrawn by the summer of 1961 when No. 65582 was captured shunting Sawston Sidings, with only eleven others along with this example to make it into the following year. (Late Vincent Heckford/Strathwood Library Collection)

Although Class 8F No. 48734 was an LMS design it was one of a number built at Darlington Works by the LNER, and in the early summer of 1961 was found wandering along the ECML near Retford as fast as it could between expresses. (Strathwood Library Collection)

Another foreigner, No. 43660 from the Midland Railway's large fleet of Class 3Fs, gets a mixed goods away from the former North Midland Railway's Rotherham Masborough station, now in the hands of the Eastern Region in 1959. (Strathwood Library Collection)

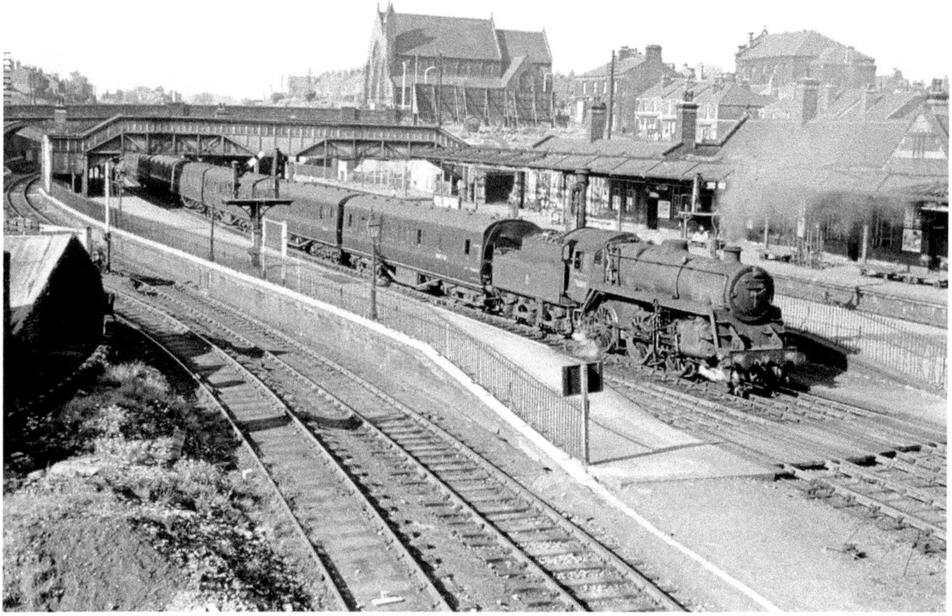

Taken shortly afterwards, a parcels train has now picked up all those mail sacks seen on the far platform in the previous view as Standard Class 4MT No. 76088 passes through on a passenger service. (Strathwood Library Collection)

Working with an open-cab Johnson Class 1F such as No. 41835, shunting at Rotherham Masborough in the summer of 1959, could be pleasant enough as long as it was not raining but in winter it was for tougher souls only no doubt. Ninety-five of these locomotives came into British Railways ownership in 1948, although their numbers were decimated by the time of this view. In fact No. 41835 was the last of its class to retain the original round-topped boiler and open cab. It was a product of the Vulcan Foundry, entering service in October 1892 and not being withdrawn until December 1966, ending its days as a shunter at Staveley Iron Works. (Strathwood Library Collection)

In contrast, Standard Class 5MT No. 73054 was built in June 1954 at Derby Works and was just five years old when it was photographed again near Rotherham Masborough in 1959, still in its original lined black livery. A much shorter eleven-year service career would befall this locomotive however, with much of its later years on the lamented Somerset & Dorset route in a lined green livery. (Strathwood Library Collection)

Another location often recalled fondly by enthusiasts was Wisbech with its tramway system. Originally there were four stations serving the town, two from the Great Eastern Railway and two from the Midland & Great Northern Railway. The last, Wisbech East, would close in 1968. On 18 October 1961, Class J20 No. 64690 was engaged in shunting the daily goods. (Late Vincent Heckford/Strathwood Library Collection)

The erection of overhead wiring masts at Seven Sisters will spell the doom of Class N7/5 No. 69664 in November 1960, and a swift cutting up two months later at Stratford Works. But on this day in the summer sunshine on 12 July 1959 its all smiles and a friendly wave from the crew as they head for Enfield. (Strathwood Library Collection)

The last of the Hill and Gresley-designed Class N7s to be built would be No. 9733, emerging from Doncaster Works in December 1928. Renumbered as No. 69733 in the summer of 1949, it would last in traffic until October 1960, when it is seen here just as the wires were going up at Walthamstow's Wood Street station. There was still a sub shed here at this time from Stratford; the main allocation of the shed was Class N7s for working suburban services to and from Liverpool Street. The shed was closed in 1960 when the line was electrified; the electric services commenced on 12 November 1960. (Colour Rail)

The busy maze of lines around Stratford's station and sheds is being passed by Class K3 No. 61970, running on the down main with an express on 7 June 1959. (Late Norman Browne/Strathwood Library Collection)

London's Docklands were still a hive of activity on 14 October 1961 when Class N7/5 No. 69640 was seen at Silvertown, although this Gorton-built tank engine from 1926 would only have eleven more months in service. (Colour Rail)

Making great haste through Haughley on 31 May 1961 was Britannia No. 70006 *Robert Burns*, which was just ten years old at the time. Both the locomotive and the station would find themselves surplus to requirements in 1967. (Strathwood Library Collection)

Another station to succumb in 1967 was Stoke, on the line through Haverhill. This was the charming scene on 24 September 1956 with Class D16/3 No. 62510 awaiting its leisurely onward run. (Dave Cobbe Collection/ Rail Photoprints)

Steam is passing through the chime whistle as No. 60015 *Quicksilver* gets away from Gainsborough Lea Road in the cold sunshine of 1 February 1962. (Colour Rail)

Gainsborough was a busy location for the railways with the Great Northern and Great Eastern having a joint station with the Great Central Railway established at Gainsborough Central. While the GN & GE established their own joint station for the town at Lea Road, both would survive the Beeching cuts. In 1964, one of Gresley's superb 184-strong Class V2s, No. 60824, was found making its way light engine through the town. (John Rowe)

Britannias such as No. 70037 *Hereward the Wake* would often find themselves heading towards Lincolnshire from London's Kings Cross, or Top Shed as it was known in the early 1960s, when they were rostered for Grimsby services while based at 40B Immingham. This view was taken in 1963, with the Britannia already coaled and prepared for the journey home from the capital. (Strathwood Library Collection)

Top Shed Interlude

Above and below: The sight of Gresley's A4s being serviced at 34A Kings Cross captivated many in the steam era, and why not indeed when we were faced with the likes of No. 60029 *Woodcock*, or No. 60034 *Lord Farringdon* and No. 60014 *Silver Link* with another unidentified streak, all on shed on 8 January 1961. Mouth-watering for any steam enthusiast, but it was not to last much longer as the shed closed here on 15 June 1963. (Both: Gerald T. Robinson)

First away on that glorious January day in 1961 was No. 60034 *Lord Farringdon*, as she moves off with her cylinder drain cocks open in a great hiss of steam in the cold winter's air. (Gerald T. Robinson)

This same Gresley Class A4 gives us a fine comparison of front ends at Top Shed in 1959, with the design of Peppercorn and his Class A1 Pacifics such as 60153 *Flamboyant*, which was built eleven years after the A4. (Colour Rail)

Another of Peppercorn's Class A1s, No. 60133 *Pommern*, is seen alongside a fellow Pacific, Gresley-designed Class A3 No. 60050 *Persimmon*, in the winter of 1962/3. (Late Vincent Heckford/Strathwood Library Collection)

A further view taken on 8 January 1961 shows No. 60013 *Dominion of New Zealand* being turned at Kings Cross shed while another Class A3, No. 60039 *Sandwich*, stands alongside. (Gerald T. Robinson)

Old King Coal

A coastal fog or haar roles in near Sunderland in the first few days of September 1967 as Class Q6 No. 63395 shuffles another rake of empties back to the collieries. This would be the final week of steam operation in the North East. (Strathwood Library Collection)

The other main ex-North Eastern Railway locomotive to survive in service at this time was the Worsdell-designed Class J27, such as No. 65804, also at the head of coal empties at Ryhope Grange on 14 June 1967. (Michael Beeton)

Running tender-first on a warm summer's day would be a pleasant experience as another Class J27, No. 65882, heads northwards at Ryhope Grange on that same warm June day in 1967. (Michael Beeton)

To enjoy the same experience on an Ivatt Class 4MT, such as No. 43123, you would have to lean out of the side windows, as here at Ashington in 1967 in a landscape unrecognisable today. (Rail Photoprints)

Coal empties are drawn through Pelaw on 15 June 1967 by Class Q6 No. 63429, one of the seventeen survivors of the 120-strong class to make it into this the last year of steam in the North East. (Michael Beeton)

A busy scene at Hartlepool in June 1967 as No. 90698 clanks and squeals around the curves and a DMU clatters away in platforms, but one railwayman strolls along in the warm sunshine. (Michael Beeton)

Shuffling around at Pelaw with safety valves blowing in July 1966 was Class 9F No. 92099 with some coal empties. This would be a leisurely break from the arduous iron ore trains on the route to Consett. (Rail Photoprints)

Two rakes of coal empties with Class J27s have just passed at Ryhope Grange as No. 65855 approaches our cameraman on 14 June 1967. Soon it would just be diesels along this coastal section of line. (Michael Beeton)

A number of photographers seized the chance to enjoy the decline of steam in the North East while they could during the last two summers in 1966 and 1967. This is the view from the platform ends at West Hartlepool on 29 June 1966 with Class Q6 during the last two summers 63407 signalled away once more on coal duties. (Gilroy A. Kerr)

More tender-first running for another Q6 just a short way away at Sunderland as No. 63395 makes some smoke with a long rake of sixteen-ton wagons this time. This would be the only one of this 120-strong class to live on in preservation. (Strathwood Library Collection)

This time it is a mixed rake of wagons for Peppercorn-designed Class K1 No. 62060 to edge forward with at Ryhope Grange, once more on that sunny 14 June 1967. This example of the seventy-strong class of Moguls was released to traffic in December 1949, from the North British workshops in Glasgow. All seventy members of the class were built within a period of just ten months, with the first withdrawn in 1962 and this locomotive being one of the last twenty-four still in traffic during 1967. (Michael Beeton)

Thanks to the North Eastern Locomotive Preservation Group's members this Class J27, No. 65894, was saved for posterity along with Class Q6 No. 63395 and Class K1 No. 62005 when steam was laid to rest on British Rail's North Eastern Region in September 1967. The well-kept No. 65894 makes a rousing start from Sunderland South Dock on 6 September 1967. (George Woods)

Above and below: Another smartly turned out Class J27 a few days later, No. 65882 has plenty of steam to spare as it passes Ryhope with coal empties to South Hetton Colliery on 8 September 1967. The colliery at South Hetton was first sunk on 1 March 1831, with coal production beginning on 5 August 1833. This Class J27 was built eighty-nine years later in 1922 at Darlington Works to a design by Wilson Worsdell, with the last thirty-five locomotives of the class at the request of Vincent Raven to his modified design. South Hetton Colliery ceased coal production in 1982. Also hard at work in 1967 that same day was No. 65894, with empties for Silksworth Colliery. This colliery opened in 1869 and closed in 1971. (Both: Gerald T. Robinson)

The storm sheet is slung over the roof of fellow Class J27 No. 65855 so that the crew can enjoy the cooling breeze and a breather as they work tender-first through Pelaw on 15 June 1967. (Michael Beeton)

This is the soon to be preserved No. 65894, once more in typical condition for these hard worked engines, on 14 June 1967 at Ryhope Grange. (Michael Beeton)

The fireman on board Austerity No. 90074 joins his driver for a view of the signals near West Hartlepool with a southbound loaded coal train on 7 September 1967. Note the prominence of television aerials. (Gerald T. Robinson)

Shed & Works Visits South

Another of the once ubiquitous War Department Austerities, No. 90246, stands in front of Class 9F No. 92183 at Peterborough's New England shed on 10 April 1960. Fellow products from North British in the shape of the Type 2 diesels would be less successful and soon head back to Glasgow. (Frank Hornby)

Taken on the same visit to New England was this busy scene by the once large coaling stage as the shed pilot for today, Class N5 No. 69293, is engaged on shunting locomotives out of steam in its last few months of operation itself. (Late Norman Browne/Strathwood Library Collection)

The large ferro-concrete coaling plant at the nearby Cambridgeshire shed at March dominates the background to No. 62530. This Class D15 was built at Stratford Works by the Great Eastern Railway in 1902 for their tightly timed mainline services, with many of these fine locomotives being rebuilt in later years on the instructions of Sir Nigel Gresley and classified as D16/3. (Colour Rail)

This large locomotive shed was closed to steam on 1 December 1963, although visiting steam engines continued to find work into the nearby marshalling yards and required servicing here. It was also a shorter term dumping ground for locomotives on their way to the breakers' yards at Norwich and Wymondham. This visit on 18 April 1960 certainly looked profitable for spotters though. (Frank Hornby)

Alongside the station platforms at Cambridge was located another former Great Eastern Railway shed with Class E4 No. 62785 being the subject of this morning's work for the cleaners. (Alan Pike OBE)

A return to 34E New England shed in 1962 to record Class A3 No. 60044 *Melton* standing by the overhead water columns. (Strathwood Library Collection)

Above and below: In 1911, Robinson introduced a most successful design of 2-8-0 for the Great Central Railway for their coal traffic. Over the next nine years 130 of these popular locomotives were built. In addition another 521 locomotives were built for the Railway Operation Division of the Royal Engineers for war service during the First World War. Some 329 of these 2-8-0s survived various modifications and rebuilds to join the British Railways fleet in 1948. A good location to enjoy them would be here at Retford, where we see two examples around 1963. Coded 36E, Retford shed consisted of two buildings, one of Great Central origin and another from the Great Northern, which were considered as one depot. The GCR portion closed in January 1965 and was smartly demolished to make way for the Retford flyunder, while the former GNR building soldiered on until closure in June 1965. (John Rowe & Strathwood Library Collection)

Above and below: Visits to Stratford depot and works would mean a large number of entries in most spotters' books and this visit on 7 June 1959 would be no exception, with Class K3 No. 61926 stabled among the many engines here that day as Britannia No. 70013 *Oliver Cromwell* edged past with its newly modified smoke deflectors. (Frank Hornby & Late Norman Browne/Strathwood Library Collection)

Further Britannias were also present that day, with 70036 *Boadicea* still retaining the original handrails to her smoke deflectors and looking less well kept, or is that woad? (Late Norman Browne/Strathwood Library Collection)

Another works and shed servicing Eastern Region locomotives were firmly in London Midland Region territory on the outskirts of Manchester at Gorton, where we find Class O4 No. 63818 recently outshopped around 1960. (Strathwood Library Collection)

The Great Northern Railway bestowed not only Sir Nigel Gresley and his genius for Pacifics upon the LNER and thus into the British Railways era, but also tank locomotives such as Class J50/1 No. 68896. While this one dates from 1914 and Doncaster Works, the last ones emerged from Gorton Works weeks before the outbreak of the Second World War. A Baby Deltic is in the background to this view at Hornsey in 1959. (Late Norman Browne/Strathwood Library Collection)

After Gresley's death on 5 April 1941 Edward Thompson took over as his successor; ironically both were educated at Marlborough Public School in Wiltshire. The first Pacifics to appear in his reign were rebuilds of Gresley's Class P2 2-8-2s. But No. 60514 *Chamossaire*, seen here at the small shed alongside the platforms at Hitchin on 4 August 1962, was to his own design as a Class A2/3. (Peter Coton)

Back to another platform-edge locomotive shed, again at Cambridge, to see Class E4 No. 62785, now fully cleaned and bulled up for railtour duty on 16 May 1959. Upon withdrawal that December she was set aside for preservation as part of the National Collection. (Frank Hornby)

Reasonably clean from its recent overhaul, Ivatt Class 4MT No. 43143 enjoys the attention of her driver at Stratford on 2 May 1960. While the Class E4 opposite gave sixty-four years' service, this Mogul built at Doncaster in 1951 was only given just under fourteen years' use before scrapping. (Colour Rail)

Doncaster Salute

Above: While the builds of the 184 Gresley-designed Class V2s were shared between Darlington and Doncaster, it would of course be a Doncaster-constructed locomotive chosen to be named *King's Own Yorkshire Light Infantry*. This is No. 60872 on shed shortly before withdrawal in September 1963, still proudly wearing her nameplates; these were very different to those later worn by the Deltic D9002. (John Rowe)

Left: Well-dressed spotters visit Doncaster's shed on 16 July 1961 and there is a chance for a look on the footplate of Class A1 No. 60161 *North British*, another product of the works here from December 1949. (Strathwood Library Collection)

Above and below: Colour photography inside the workshops was difficult due to the lighting conditions, but to get an elevated view such as this is quite rare. We do not know who the cameraman was but assume him to have been a member of staff here who fortunately recorded a number of superb images for us. This one depicts Class A3s Nos 60044 *Melton* and 60108 *Gay Crusader* receiving light repairs in late 1962 while Class A1 No. 60130 *Kestrel* has received a full overhaul and is being admired by some of the works fitters about the same time. (Both Strathwood Library Collection)

The smokebox of No. 60009 *Union of South Africa* has been left open after a quick clean-out and inspection in the works yard before repairs inside the workshops in early 1961. (Strathwood Library Collection)

Withdrawn in April 1963, No. 60022 *Mallard* was given a cosmetic restoration back to full streamlined condition and released in February 1964 to go on display at Clapham Transport Museum. (Strathwood Library Collection)

Above and below: The future would be less promising for Class A2/3 No. 60526 *Sugar Palm*, dumped alongside the works in late 1962 after being withdrawn in October. North British-built Austerity No. 90275 would enjoy a few more months' work after this visit in early 1963, until July 1965 at least. (Both: Strathwood Library Collection)

Above and below: A view down at workshop level inside Doncaster Works this time as Class K1 No. 62058 undergoes overhaul with what looks like an A1 and a B1 for company, and not a diesel or an electric in sight. Another cosmetic restoration for display in preservation for No. 60008 *Dwight D. Eisenhower* in early 1964, although this A4 would go on display much further away than Clapham. Instead it was destined for Wisconsin in the United States of America. (Both: Strathwood Library Collection)

Eventually 409 Thompson-designed Class B1s would be built at Darlington and by North British, but the Vulcan Foundry built fifty examples including No. 61188, ex-works after overhaul around 1962. (Strathwood Library Collection)

Finally, we could not leave Doncaster without another view of perhaps its second most famous locomotive, No. 60022 *Mallard*, on shed at 36A close to the end of her service days. (P.J. Hughes/Colour Rail)

Through the Links North

No high visibility vests at Wakefield Kirkgate for this two-man track gang on 21 August 1964 as Austerities Nos 90210 and 90353 put in appearances today. (Douglas Twibble)

Still in original condition as Fowler had designed his Patriot Class of 4-6-0s, No. 45513 was photographed at Leeds Central in 1962, its last year in traffic. (Strathwood Library Collection)

Some more Austerity action at Wakefield Kirkgate 2 January 1967 as No. 90363 ambles through while a couple of guards enjoy the winter sunshine on the veranda of their brake van. (Bill Wright)

Winter sunshine again on 17 March 1957, but things look a little more serious for the departure of No. 60020 *Guillemot* from York with an express. (Colour Rail)

There is a large platform gathering for the departure of today's down working of the Thames–Clyde Express away from Leeds City on 5 September 1961. Holbeck shed has done little work on appearance in their preparation of Class A3 No. 60088 *Book Law*. (Douglas Twibble)

Likewise, the turn-out of Jubilee No. 45573 *Newfoundland* on a stopping service at Keighley in 1963 does little to raise the spirits, although we suspect the sound of its exhaust storming away from here would bring a smile to any enthusiast for steam. (Strathwood Library Collection)

Another view of No. 92063, first seen on page 13, working hard on her climb through South Pelaw in the mid-1960s with further Class 9 power from yet another of these Tyne Dock-allocated Class 9Fs banking hard behind on one of the once important Consett iron ore workings. (Noel Marrison)

Its early morning still on 30 April 1966 and Fairburn Class 4MT No. 42093 is engaged on warming the coaches through while they are still being serviced at Bradford Hammerton Street, while her fireman engages in a little coal trimming. (Win Wall/Strathwood Library Collection)

Bradford's other large station was Exchange, which was opened by the Lancashire & Yorkshire Railway and the Great Northern Railway on 9 May 1850. Steam is plentiful in this early morning view of Stanier Class 4MT No. 42616 with the 07.45 through coaches for Yarmouth Vauxhall on 22 July 1967. (Ian Turnbull/ Rail Photoprints)

Two Class J72s were painted in LNER apple green livery and used as station pilots at York and Newcastle. Both were built by Armstrong Whitworth in 1922. One was No. 68736 and this one, No. 68723, rests between duties at Newcastle station on 13 March 1962. (Gerald T. Robinson)

The power stations that once stood either side of the River Tyne at Stella have now gone, but on 2 November 1965 they were a significant backdrop to Class J27 No. 65796 shunting the yard. (Strathwood Library Collection)

Before the Class 9Fs took over their duties, Tyne Dock shed provided Class O1s such as No. 63760, seen here in 1957 as it clambers past South Pelaw with a Tyne Dock to Consett iron ore working. (Dave Cobbe Collection/Rail Photoprints)

Leeds City station was much rebuilt during the early 1960s, with traffic diverted from Leeds Central station, allowing its closure. The last workings of Leeds Holbeck shed's Jubilees on trains for Carlisle were very popular among enthusiasts by September 1966, where we see No. 45647 *Sturdee* all bulled up with white paint at least, if still more than a little grimy. (Michael Beeton)

Similar treatment with white paintwork was afforded to Class V2 No. 60885, seen running light engine out of Leeds City station on 20 July 1963, perhaps for a recent enthusiasts' special. In the background spotters sit on the platforms in the warm sunshine while at least two Black Fives are seen in the distance. (Rail Photoprints)

The white smokebox hinges can just be made out underneath all the filth on Britannia No. 70053 *Moray Firth*, now bereft of its nameplates too on 27 March 1967, with a Glasgow relief at Leeds City standing at platform 12. (Douglas Twibble)

It's all aboard for the crews of Class V3 No. 67652 and Class V1 No. 67647 at Newcastle Central in 1956 for what seems an unusual working for these locomotives built at Doncaster to Gresley's design. (Dave Cobbe Collection/Rail Photoprints)

A much cleaner Class A3 No. 60088 *Book Law*, this time leaving Newcastle Central with a vans train in February 1961 after a light fall of snow. (Gerald T. Robinson)

Snow has not put off the spotters at Darlington on 12 January 1963, as No. 60022 *Mallard* has pulled in with a Glasgow to Kings Cross service. (Strathwood Library Collection)

Doomed

The scrapping area at Doncaster Works would get through a large number of steam, diesel and even a few electric locomotives over the years, some glamorous and many workaday such as this Gresley trio, led by Class J50/2 No. 68929 with classes N2 and K3 behind, in 1961. (Strathwood Library Collection)

It looks like the nameplate bolts for No. 60024 *Kingfisher* did not come cleanly from this view of it standing awaiting cutting up at North Blyth in October 1966. Just a short while beforehand it had been at work on a number of enthusiasts' specials, far from its regular haunts on the Southern and Western regions. (Strathwood Library Collection)

The end approaches for Class J19 No. 64664 at Stratford in 1962, having just been withdrawn in September. (Strathwood Library Collection)

Likewise, Class N7 No. 69642 would soon perish like so many locomotives here at Stratford. It was withdrawn in November 1960. (Frank Hornby)

Posted as withdrawn days later, Class D16/3 No. 62517 will not leave Stratford again after this view in August 1959 as it was cut up here that November after fifty-eight years of loyal service. (Late Norman Browne/ Strathwood Library Collection)

With so many steam locomotives to dispose of, British Railways' works could no longer cope by the early sixties, resulting in scenes such as this at Station Steel's yard at Wath on 26 June 1966. Nos 63781 and 63653 are alongside Class 9F No. 92115, withdrawn with less than ten years' service. (Strathwood Library Collection)

With affectionate chalked markings, Austerity No. 90644 stands among other condemned locomotives at Normanton on 23 July 1967. It would be moved for scrapping that autumn to Arnott Young's scrapyard at Parkgate. (Gerald T. Robinson)

The contents of the melancholy scraplines at South Blyth shed are being freely examined by spotters on 19 February 1967, with a mix of Class K1s, Ivatt Moguls and an Austerity visible in this view. (Colin Rodgers/Strathwood Library Collection)

Class V2 No. 60931 is the next locomotive in line for the cutters at the Shipbreakers Yard at Dunston on Bonfire Night in 1965 after an unknown classmate alongside has been dealt with. (Strathwood Library Collection)

The tender may still have coal in it but all the plates from Class A1 No. 60121 *Silurian* have already vanished in the same month that it was posted as withdrawn from here at York shed in October 1965. (John Gill)

Shed & Works Visits North

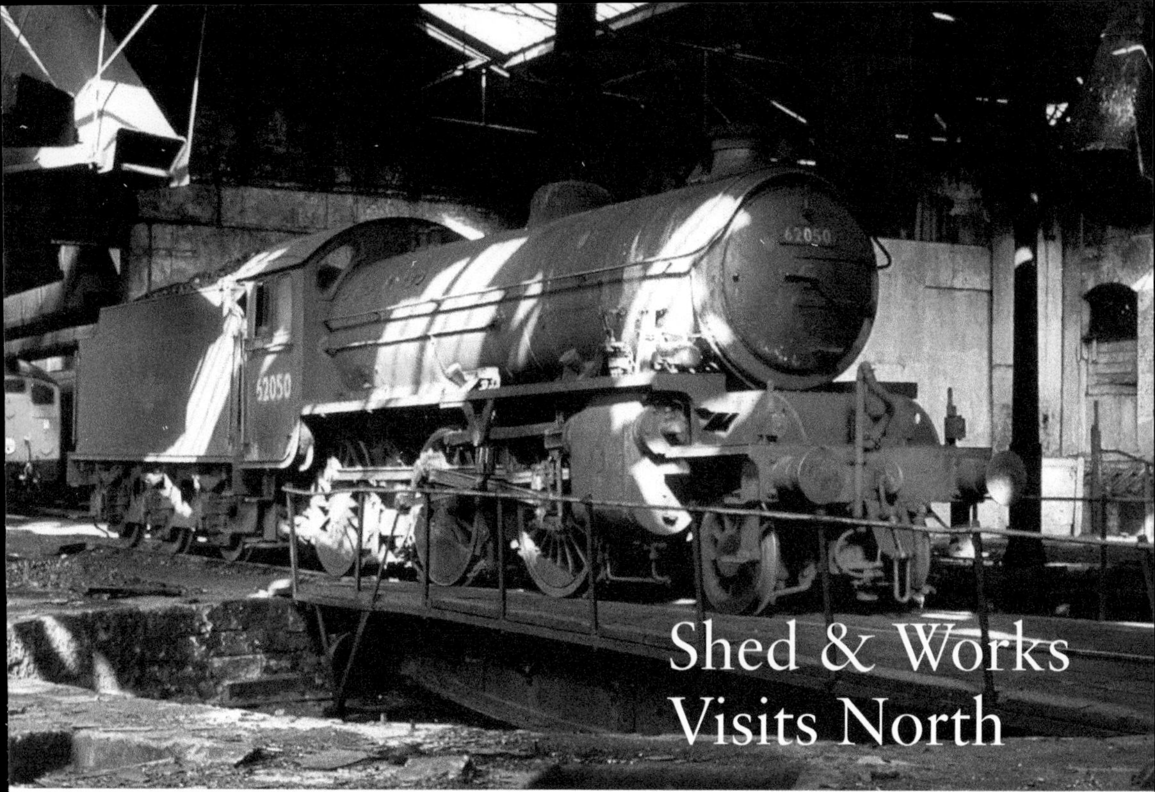

Tyne Dock shed had closed to steam on 1 September 1967, leaving Class K1 No. 62050 stuck inside out of steam among the diesels which would continue using Tyne Dock as a stabling point only until 28 February 1970. (George Woods)

A diesel fuel tank has already been provided at 55D Royston shed and can be seen beyond the row of Stanier 8Fs still present on 20 May 1967. Royston shed would close to steam on 4 November 1967 with total closure being effected on 26 September 1971. (Jerry Beddows)

When steam finished at 55A Holbeck on 1 December 1967 the wonderfully evocative roundhouse would be demolished, leaving the diesels outside. This is Jubilee No. 45562 *Alberta*, which sadly did not make it to preservation during those last few months of steam in Leeds. (Jim Winkley)

The fireman has jumped out to walk alongside and set any required points for his driver on this Vulcan Foundry-built Black Five, No. 45080, seen shuffling about in the shed yard at Holbeck on 30 May 1967. (Strathwood Library Collection)

The cylinder drain cocks hiss furiously on Class Q6 No. 63387 moving off shed at West Hartlepool, probably for the very last time under its own power, on 7 September 1967. (Gerald T. Robinson)

There is not much sign of live steam here at Low Moor shed on 9 April 1967 as Fairburn Class 4MT No. 42055 and Black Five No. 44695 stand about in the drizzle. (Gerald T. Robinson)

Both smoke and steam emanate from Class A7 No. 69784 at 53D Hull Springhead in May 1955. The rundown shed buildings had been built by the Hull & Barnsley Railway and they would close completely on 1 December 1958. (Trevor Owen/Colour Rail)

Ash, spilt coal and the general rubbish from a shed yard can be seen strewn all about Class K1 No. 62022 at North Blyth shed while an outside cylinder 0-6-0ST from the National Coal Board runs alongside on 7 August 1965. (Tony Butcher)

One of the large batch of North British-built Class B1s, No. 61199 runs light engine alongside 50A York during September 1965, this example being withdrawn just five months before the shed closed to steam on 25 June 1967. (John Gill)

We hope all that smoke stops once Class 9F No. 92168 has made it inside the roundhouses at York around 1964. The working life of this Crewe-built 2-10-0 was a scandalously short seven and half years! (Colour Rail)

Above and below: Black Five No. 45051 keeps company with some of the diesels which now operated most of the former North Eastern Region's services in York's shed yard in June 1966. Meanwhile, five years beforehand Class A2/3 No. 60514 *Chamossaire* could be seen waiting for access to the turntable here. (Both: John Gill)

Above and below: Class K1 No. 62042 joins Class 9F No. 92173 and Class A1 No. 60124 *Kenilworth* out by the coaler at York in 1965. On the same day, nearby in York's extensive shed yard, was one of Tyne Dock's air pump-fitted Class 9Fs, No. 92061, having brought a freight south. (Both: Douglas Paul)

Next, a trip on 8 April 1966 to the home of those 9Fs at Tyne Dock, but today we find Class K1 No. 62007 keeping company with Class Q6 No. 63431 inside the shed during an enthusiasts' visit. (George Woods)

Keeping alive Gateshead's reputation for filthy locomotives, we see Class V2 No. 60904 taking on water alongside an equally scruffy Peak diesel on 8 September 1963. (Strathwood Library Collection)

Also on shed at Gateshead on 8 September 1963, wearing the perhaps flimsy looking train reporting number of a special affixed to one of its front lamp irons, was Class A1 No. 60150 *Willbrook*. (Strathwood Library Collection)

We catch up with the apple green-liveried Class J72 No. 68723 once again at Gateshead where it looks to be carrying considerable signs of pollution and soot around its dome on 17 August 1963. (Strathwood Library Collection)

There is no polished brass safety bonnet cover and fancy green livery for fellow classmate No. 69025 in the shed yard at 52A Gateshead in 1962. This Class J72 was built as recently as April 1951 at Darlington Works by British Railways. (Strathwood Library Collection)

A Drewry shunter has just emerged from the workshops in about 1964 after overhaul here at Darlington Works, where the Class J72 opposite was built less than a decade earlier. Also on show ex-works are Standard Class 4MT No. 75062 and an unknown Class K1 and a Class J94. (Noel Marrison)

An ex-works Stanier 8F stands in the shed yard at Darlington in during 1965 in the April sunshine while a somewhat dusty Class A1 No. 60124 *Kenilworth* puts in another appearance, drifting its steam across the shed yard. (Strathwood Library Collection)

Out by the ash pits at Darlington's shed on 13 May 1962, Maunsell's Schools Class No. 30925 *Cheltenham* is prepared alongside Class 2P No. 40646 for their return run to Nottingham Victoria, with the RCTS arranged 'East Midlander No. 5' railtour. (Strathwood Library Collection)

Specials

A number of specials were run into former LNER territory by No. 7029 *Clun Castle* during the mid-1960s as the locomotive's owner, Pat Whitehouse, sought to get his locomotive to pay for its upkeep and to support other preservationists. Today on 30 September 1967 the Castle will take over from D1503, which will bring passengers from Kings Cross, and take them on to Carlisle, where the now preserved No. 4498 *Sir Nigel Gresley* will bring them back to meet up with the same Brush Type 4 for their return to Kings Cross. But first engine preparation at New England shed for *Clun Castle*, with lots of coal and a full tender of water, together with a clean fire. (Strathwood Library Collection)

Arrival has been made at Peterborough East station from St Pancras behind Royal Scot Class No. 46155 *The Lancer* on 19 September 1964. From here Class A1 No. 60128 *Bongrace* will take the LCGB's Pennine Limited Rail Tour onwards to Sheffield Victoria and the next engine change of the day. Four further changeovers would take place before No. 46155 *The Lancer* met up with the tour once more at Nottingham Victoria for the return, to London's Marylebone station this time. (Frank Hornby)

Tour passengers roam free-range around Stoke Ferry after arriving behind Class J69/1 No. 68566 on 12 July 1959 on the LCGB's Eastern Counties Rail Tour. (Strathwood Library Collection)

Austerity No. 90445 stands at Harton with an SLS Brake Van special from West Hartlepool to Tyne Dock and local branches on 15 May 1965. (Chris Davies/Rail Photoprints)

Another SLS tour run in conjunction with the RCTS was their mammoth five-day North Eastern Tour of 1963 which involved at least ten locomotives. One of these was Ivatt Class 4MT No. 43057, which is seen here at Amble on 29 September 1963. (Strathwood Library Collection)

On 20 May 1967 the SLS ran their Three Dales Rail Tour using the soon to be preserved Class K1 No. 62005 throughout. However, D5160 was required as the crossing loop at Redmire was not long enough to accommodate the six-coach train, as seen here at Leyburn. (Strathwood Library Collection)

Another sparkling clean Class K1, No. 62027, changes over with the preserved Class Q7 No. 63460 on 28 September 1963 at Consett, once again on that mammoth SLS/RCTS North Eastern Tour, 1963. Again tour passengers roam freely trackside to get their pictures, before re-joining their train. (Strathwood Library Collection)

On 9 May 1964, Stanier's Duchess No. 46251 *City of Nottingham* makes a lovely spectacle at Charwelton on the former Great Central Railway's route to London, which was part of the Eastern Region during the previous decade but was by this time in the hands of the London Midland Region, who wanted rid of it. (Dave Cobbe Collection/Rail Photoprints)

Another Stanier engine, Jubilee Class No. 45593 *Kolhapur*, is almost ready to depart for Carlisle from Bradford Forster Square on 30 April 1966 with the Jubilee Railway Society's South Yorkshireman No. 5 Rail Tour. (Win Wall/Strathwood Library Collection)

Class B1 No. 61360 waits under the wires at Sheffield Victoria on 27 June 1964, at the start of the RCTS IGH Peak Rail Tour. (Strathwood Library Collection)

Twenty-six miles out on this same RCTS tour on 27 June 1964, and the pioneer Class EM1, E26000 *Tommy*, is put on as a pilot for the run through the infamous Woodhead Tunnel to Guide Bridge. The Thompson-designed B1 would then carry on alone to Parsley Hay where Nos 68012, 68079 and 47006 would take passengers in open wagons on a tour of the High Peak lines. Passengers would then meet up once more with No. 61360 at High Peak Junction for their return to Sheffield Victoria after a 144-mile tour. (Strathwood Library Collection)

Almost exactly twice the tour mileage would be enjoyed by participants of the Stephenson Locomotive Society and Manchester Locomotive Society's Ashington Rail Tour on 10 June three years later in 1967. Black Five No. 45428 would start the day at Huddersfield, giving way to Jubilee No. 45562 *Alberta* at York for the run to Ashington. Here the train joined the NCB's network for a run to Lynmouth and back behind the system's No. 39 in a rake of ancient ex North Eastern Railway coaches. Meanwhile, the Jubilee waited for their return underneath the extensive overhead coal slag cableways that once fed the largest slagheap in Europe. (Strathwood Library Collection)

Above and below: The ECS working for the Stephenson Locomotive Society's Three Dales Rail Tour on 20 May 1967 stops briefly at West Hartlepool in glorious sunshine. However, not all railtours were blessed with fine weather, as here with the RCTS Great Eastern Suburban Rail Tour in the rain at Enfield Town behind Class J69/1 number 68619 on 12 November 1960. (Both: Strathwood Library Collection)

Above and below: We are blessed with sunshine for the changeover between Class J17 No. 65567 and Britannia No. 70003 *John Bunyan* at Thetford on 31 March 1962 while working the RCTS Great Eastern Commemorative Steam Rail Tour. (Both: Strathwood Library Collection)

On 19 September 1965 the RCTS ran their Blyth & Tyne Rail Tour, utilising No. 60004 *William Whitelaw*. Unfortunately for tour participants, English Electric Type 3 D6769 was put on at Eaglescliffe. This was because the A4 was banned from the Stockton & Darlington direct line due to the poor condition of this route. Although a Class K1 was expected to be used north of the Tyne, it was Ivatt Class 4MT No. 43057 that was substituted. Meanwhile Class A1 No. 60124, now running without its *Kenilworth* nameplates, was acting as standby. Its duty completed without being called upon, it now prepares to leave Stockton and return to Darlington. (Chris Davies/Rail Photoprints)

Another railtour that almost ended in failure was on 2 July 1967, when the SLS ran their Electric/Steam Rail Tour from Birmingham New Street to Stockport behind an AC electric locomotive. Here Britannia No. 70038, with painted-on *Robin Hood* nameplates, took over for what was hoped to be a good run to here at York, where we see the Pacific backing on for the return run after everyone had been given an official visit to 50A York shed. Unfortunately steam operation here had concluded the previous month but there were some stored locomotives to be seen in the yard. To make matters worse the runs behind the Britannia were best described as poor, the brakes coming on two or three times at least on the return run, possibly due to a lack of vacuum. But on this occasion there was no back-up steam locomotive available so the engine crew had to press on regardless. (Strathwood Library Collection)

Having made the fifty-seven miles from Liverpool Street to here at Witham in a leisurely ninety-one minutes on 10 August 1958, Class J19 No. 64656 rests for twelve minutes before completing the last eight miles of its duty onwards to Marks Tey. Here Class J15 No. 65440 would be waiting to take over for an equally easy ramble along the Colne Valley line to Cambridge. (Strathwood Library Collection)

Back once more to the SLS The Dales Rail Tour on 20 May 1967. The weather had changed from the glorious sunshine of the morning to rainfall by the time Bishop Auckland was reached later in the afternoon. At the time the tour was originally planned it was thought there would no longer be watering facilities at Darlington or here at Bishop Auckland, and it was anticipated that a change to diesel power would be enforced on the journey up to Weardale. Good fortune shone even if the sun now refused to as the locomotive change was not required and 62005 watered at Darlington Bank Top on the outward and here on the return. (Strathwood Library Collection)

Above and below: To conclude, we see what was advertised as the Farewell to A3 Rail Tour on 5 June 1965 with No. 60052 *Prince Palatine* at Newcastle Central while a few weeks earlier on 10 April cameramen were out in force to record No. 4472 *Flying Scotsman* through Peterborough on a private charter run by Alan Pegler to thank the British Railways staff who had overhauled his A3. (Strathwood Library Collection & Michael Beeton)